Running WILD

More Than Scars

KATHERINE FRIESE, MSN, APRN, CNP

WESTBOW
PRESS®
A DIVISION OF THOMAS NELSON
& ZONDERVAN

WestBow Press books may be ordered through booksellers or by contacting:

WestBow Press
A Division of Thomas Nelson & Zondervan
1663 Liberty Drive
Bloomington, IN 47403
www.westbowpress.com
1 (866) 928-1240

Because of the dynamic nature of the Internet, any web addresses or
links contained in this book may have changed since publication and
may no longer be valid. The views expressed in this work are solely those
of the author and do not necessarily reflect the views of the publisher,
and the publisher hereby disclaims any responsibility for them.

Any people depicted in stock imagery provided by Getty Images are
models, and such images are being used for illustrative purposes only.
Certain stock imagery © Getty Images.

Scripture quotations are taken from the Holy Bible, New Living
Translation, copyright ©1996, 2004, 2015 by Tyndale House Foundation.
Used by permission of Tyndale House Publishers, a Division of Tyndale
House Ministries, Carol Stream, Illinois 60188. All rights reserved.

ISBN: 978-1-9736-9693-3 (sc)
ISBN: 978-1-9736-9692-6 (hc)
ISBN: 978-1-9736-9694-0 (e)

Library of Congress Control Number: 2020912988

Print information available on the last page.

WestBow Press rev. date: 07/21/2020

Dedicated to the cancer warriors and
those who love and care for them.
In loving memory of Sarah Stelzner.
To Brad, Blake, and Norah: I love you.

Contents

Section 3: Recovery

Preface

This is my story; you have your own. May this book offer inspiration, hope, and strength on your journey. I started writing immediately after my diagnosis of breast cancer just after my fortieth birthday. I had so much to say about my life leading up to this point and how it would help me beat cancer. In this book, I share significant life struggles to show how adversity develops endurance, strength of character, and hope. *Running Wild: More Than Scars* chronicles my cancer journey and observations along the way. My writing began as a mission to encourage and inform; it became a cornerstone to my healing. I strive to demonstrate that we are not defined by our challenges, but we are rather transformed by them.

I'm a health-care provider and am uniquely positioned to write this book as a professional and a cancer survivor. Please remember, this publication is not intended as a substitute for the advice of your health-care professionals.

Acknowledgments

Thank you to my health-care teams at Sanford Joe Lueken Cancer Center and Sanford Roger Maris Cancer Center, my family, my friends, WestBow Press for your guidance, Kirby Photography for cover images, Mary McCracken for your utmost encouragement, and author William Mohn for reading my work and referring me to WestBow Press. Your love and support has meant the world to me. I am truly grateful. Thank you also to creatives, musicians, and big brave thinkers. Your light inspires me.

Introduction

Running Wild

I'm tempted not to tell you the full story. My strength is returning, and so is the human tendency to put up smokescreens. Hiding my vulnerability would keep me from being completely honest and prevent me from giving you my "me too." Me too—I have struggled and overcome, fallen and stood up, experienced loss and then healing, and all the messiness in between. Cancer will break you down, stripping every ounce of pride and constructed assurance, yet at the same time show what a warrior you really are. Yep, this book is about cancer, the Big C, and so much more. Can you handle it? This is my fight song.

My calendar reads March 19, 2018, mastectomy; March 26–29, write book. I had so much to say about my life and the fire burning inside after learning I had cancer. I wrote without inhibition—after all, I might die. The book would be a gift I'd leave behind. I wouldn't have to answer questions or live with the uneasiness of people knowing too much about me.

But what if I didn't die? Why do we hold back while we live? I found stepping close to death does so much for living. It breaks the mundane, the assumed progression from one day to the next. I hold on to that terrifying time, living with the unknown, but also living in love, surrender, and spontaneity.

The cancer journey, as many call it, aligns itself with an analogy of an endurance event. A marathon has an extensive training phase, the race, and then recovery. Life, with all its ups and downs, joys and losses, struggles and successes prepares one for that race. At race time, it is all on you, but it's not all you. It is your race but made easier to endure by friends and strangers who offer encouragement. Recovery starts with complete mental, emotional, and physical exhaustion. Recovery happens slowly and opens the possibility for building back stronger than before. I'm not dead. I have so much to say about that.

Section 1

Training

Wild

"How are you holding up?" Boss Lady asked with pensive eyes. It was the morning after I learned of the cancer diagnosis.

"Great, actually. And no, I'm not being sarcastic. I feel like a wild animal out of control that is ready to kick some serious cancer!"

I drove to work that morning, jamming to a Latin song that I don't know the words to, but it has a rhythm that tells me it's about living and surviving. My spirit was ablaze, and I craved life like never before.

Rachel, dumbfounded that I even presented to work, said, "You've got to be the strongest person I know."

I'm sure they all thought I fell off my rocker. Quite simply, I needed to be present with people. That is why I was there. It had been a rough week of callbacks for more testing, meetings with specialists, poor sleep, and then the passing of my dear father-in-law.

I slept the whole night after a multitude of early mornings with tears streaming down my face. Sometimes the clock showed four a.m.; other times it read just after midnight. I contemplated the impacts of my death, specifically for my husband and two young children. That frightened me the most.

One early morning, I felt comforted by the warm presence of my feisty female line, women both passed and living. They reminded me of where I come from—a line of strong women. And then I heard my dear sweet father, gone from his physical being nearly half my life. He called me by my childhood nickname, saying, "Go get 'em, Kate Kid." My entire life I've been training for this event, this moment.

Flashbacks 2

"When will I ever get breasts?" fourteen-year-old me asked my mother.

"Oh, Katie, it's quite a disadvantage to have large breasts."

This was, of course, an unsatisfactory response. I never grew into having much of a chest, yet I became quite content being a grown women with size 32A breasts. Size A never caused the physical or emotional pain that comes with being seen as a sexual object. I was strong and unhindered. Though my tummy stuck out to match my bound breasts in a tight sports bra, I was not required to lug anything larger than size A around on back-country camping trips, unending yards in the pool, and mile upon mile on foot. I knew a mastectomy would not be a huge deal because I wouldn't look much different. More importantly, my womanhood was not based on the size of my breasts.

Would I reconstruct? "Take it slowly," I told myself. I needed to honor what was taking place. I anticipated needing space to grieve. If I woke from surgery having a new set, what good would that do for me? What good would that hold for women with rigid definitions of beauty? Is reconstruction what I wanted, or is it what society expects a woman to want? Perhaps I could be that woman in the locker room for which other women and girls could say, "That is beautiful too."

I think about my jaw surgery at eighteen years of age, to correct a prominent jawline and crossbite resulting from a jaw that grew slightly longer on one side. My dad who was a dentist could tell early on that my teeth were not matching up. By eighteen I had stopped growing and surgery was appropriate. Surgery was a way of preventing temporomandibular joint dysfunction (TMJ). It is a gruesome surgery, one my father never thought he'd see his daughter wheeled into. My experience after surgery showed me that our minds are powerful and that they can misconstrue reality, interpreting information largely through patterns of anticipated information. So when looking in the mirror following jaw surgery, I cried. The person my mind saw did not match the image reflecting back.

The old image was me, but I didn't necessarily like what my eyes saw now. I wasn't used to seeing myself looking so symmetrical. I wondered if I'd have a similar reaction to a mastectomy where my mind and eyes disagreed.

I was an angry, anxious, and impatient teen that summer. I was supposed to be living at home in anticipation of college. I spent the summer wired completely shut, struggling to communicate and eat. I scribbled my thoughts and needs in a notebook and passed it along. This was well before text messaging.

Eating was a challenge. My mom declared to her already-thin adolescent, "Your only job this summer is to eat!"

Because of the braces, mouth plate, and wires, the only space to squeeze in food and liquid was behind the very back teeth. By threading a catheter tube attached to the end of a large syringe, I injected all sorts of nastiness.

Little did I appreciate the serious implications of a compromised airway from a mouth wired shut for six weeks. Out of pure determination, stubbornness, and lack of reason, I did not carry my wire clippers. If cutting wires meant starting over and living longer in this impaired state, I wasn't having it. I would not endure another moment wired shut. If puking was to be, it would have to come out my nose. I never puked. Thank God! I also pulled antics like swimming across the river. I lacked sensibility but owned abundant will and determination.

Grit

G rit is ultimate perseverance. Angela Lee Duckworth, educator, psychologist, and theorist, is the developer of grit theory. She explains that doing well in school and in life is not simply the result of natural talent or ease of learning. "Grit is having stamina. Grit is sticking with your future, day in, day out, not just for the week, not just for the month, but for years, and working really hard to make that future a reality" (Duckworth 2013, 3:01). Grit and resiliency develop from a growth mind-set.

Growth mind-set is the brainchild of Carol Dweck from Stanford University. Dweck explains that talents and abilities develop through practice, persistence, and effort (2014). Cameron Lisey and John Rankin-McCabe (2014) from the Charlton School Film Productions created a straightforward and touching explanation/illustration of the growth mind-set theory. A growth mind-set looks at failure and learns from it; a growth mind-set moves forward through challenges. In essence, "I may not have succeeded yet, but I will" (Lisey and Rankin-McCabe).

Growth mind-set and grit showed up early in my life. Despite my mightiest efforts, preschool me was left in the dust, trailing well behind my friends. We were assigned the task of hopping on one foot around the classroom and back to the carpeted area beneath the rocking chair. I couldn't stand on one foot, much less hop on one.

"I've seen floppy kids like this before," my pediatrician grandfather said. "Leave her alone," he suggested to my mother. "She'll catch up with her peers by the time she's ten."

Best advice ever! Never did I see myself as broken or lacking, just someone needing to work extra hard. Not only did I have catching up to do physically, but I was a late bloomer in general.

Spelling, reading, and math weren't easy. I wasn't a star student, and I sensed it. Most Improved Student was like a consolation prize. To those who did not believe in me, I say, "Shame on you! Look at me now!" To those who did, I'm eternally grateful.

Social skills, imagination, music, and swimming were my strengths. Swimming is where I felt whole and free. I could swim better than anyone my age. There was a breath-holding competition as part of the swimming unit in physical education. As early as first grade, I would hold my breath and think, *I wonder if everyone is up yet; I don't want them to think I've drowned.* I'd proudly walk away with the Tootsie Roll Pop prize.

I was labeled a late bloomer, daydreamer, and an attention deficit disorder (ADHD) sufferer. I've always hated labels—they're meant to box in, stifle, and set apart. I only partially accepted those identifiers, and I specifically aimed to disprove the ADHD identifier. I was told at one point I'd outgrown ADHD; it really doesn't matter because everyone is on a continuum. I built coping tools and worked hard out of fear of failing. Then, in college, something happened; I excelled. I'm not the only one to do better in college than in years prior. I did better in a setting where I set my own pace, my own goals, and worked uninterrupted and independently.

People with ADHD have a superpower, which is the ability to hyperfocus. This superpower hunkers down and holds on with complete and single-minded determination. Hyperfocus is also a trait that runs strong in my family. I'll own this part. It has made me so gritty.

Grit would certainly not fail me now, even in the face of cancer. Like a wild animal, I was determined to hunt this cancer down. My life would be as normal as I could make it. I refused to be sick. I had a similar experience when admitted to the hospital early for leaking amniotic fluid just prior to the due date of Blake, my first child. Labor needed to be induced. The doctor declared that I was officially sick.

"Am I? Or am I just having a baby?" I questioned. I wasn't looking for a reason to be sick.

Because I wasn't "sick," I hopped back on that treadmill five days postmastectomy. I planned to defy the image of the sick cancer patient, challenging these ideas just by showing up. Cancer will foster grit, and a lifetime of grittiness shines in the face of challenge.

Heartache 4

Two months prior to the diagnosis of invasive ductal carcinoma with scattered areas of ductal carcinoma in situ, I turned to my husband and said, "There is nothing I can't overcome."

I referred to the heartache of my struggles but also depressions—the trapping, deep, dark, and numbing type—that I have overcome. Two episodes taught me valuable lessons as I healed from both. The first depression came at age twenty-one, when my father died by suicide after years of depression. I tried hard to serve as the family peacemaker, trying to be sweet enough to coax him out of his ongoing depression. This doesn't work. Sweetness cannot change something clinical.

I was absolutely numb to the bone-deep in grief. I grieved my own loss and the sadness that had blinded his sight. He had so many gifts. Feelers feel deeply. He was a feeler and a thinker. He got caught up in his head with poor coping tools. Isolation is never good. He struggled to move on from past hurts. I grieved his hurts, many that occurred before my time. He didn't move forward from the divorce more than a decade prior, and was a player in the icy relationship that followed. I grieved not being able to call him or share my young life unfolding.

Here's the thing: love never dies. Life moves along, and joys have a way of filling the voids. I plugged along, delving into my college coursework. For me, this was coping. I graduated from University of Wisconsin-River Falls, with a bachelor's degree in elementary education and a health education minor. I did extremely well in my coursework that allowed me to create, guide, and dream. My degree was a way of undoing the wrongs inflicted on me as a young learner. I loved the idea of teaching, nurturing young minds, and developing the individual. Little was I prepared for the students who didn't move along willingly and caused disruption.

Classrooms easily become chaotic. They are full of distractions and interruptions. Students present to school with baggage and unmet needs that hinder learning. I can't blame them. I blame a system that places test sores and measurements above life-skills and well-being.

By student teaching time, my identity was firmly cemented as an educator. The more miserable I became, the more I wanted out. I eventually opted out. That decision came with my unraveling. I was completely shattered. This depression was worse than the first, because unlike my father's death, this was seemingly my fault. Now I had to rebuild myself. I vowed that never again would I place my identity in anything other than my status with God.

I took a course to become a certified nursing assistant (CNA) and worked in a nursing home for a short time. I surrendered to the idea that this could be my life. Tough love is what I needed. I was living in the safety of my mother's home. She caught on and said I could not live at home and work as a CNA for the rest of my life. I wasn't moving forward.

Because I excelled at the school thing, I enrolled in the nursing program at The College of Saint Scholastica. I choose this school because of its reputable nursing program and because Duluth, Minnesota, is situated on Lake Superior. I grew up with this lake, living north on its shore. Walks along that lake helped me heal from two major losses, one after the next.

My nursing degree took me to the Mayo Clinic. After working there for two years, I wanted more. I got a puppy, a fox-red Labrador, who I named London. I then met and married my husband and moved away. I started a master's program while working and graduated; I became a nurse practitioner. That is a fraction of my identity and much more of a tool for the work God has called me to do, for the person I am.

Neurofibromatosis Type 1

A large café au lait macule (CAL) birthmark below my left armpit was the source of my mother's concern and my grandfather's counsel. "The floppy child will overcome" became the mantra. Not until age thirty-one did I learn the word neurofibromatosis (NF).

While pregnant with my son, I developed soft bumps on the lateral aspect of my thighs and superficial irregularities on my abdomen, seen when light grazed my body just right. Small CAL freckles increased in number at my armpits, breasts, and groin. This resulted from the hormone increases related to pregnancy.

At a dermatology appointment after Blake was born, I asked, "By the way, what are these on my upper leg?"

"By-the-ways" are not how health-care providers want to end an office visit. An excision of a lesion reveled a neurofibroma and led to an official diagnosis. *Huh! What does this mean? I've been living with this my entire life and didn't know!?* The reality of the diagnosis was poignant. All of a sudden I felt set apart.

Earlier developmental struggles were likely a result of neurofibromatosis. The delayed gross motor development, early learning challenges, crooked jaw, slight scoliosis, and multiple CALs were manifestations. However, I would not let a fancy label, neurofibromatosis, rob me from being absolutely present for my two-month-old son. I would not let this new diagnosis rob me of my validity, value, and success, my uniqueness and contributions. This new label would not reduce me. One thing was for sure: I was not broken! Only things that are fixable are broken. Genes are not one of those things.

I wondered how earlier knowledge of this diagnosis would have changed my life. Caring for individuals with neurofibromatosis forty years ago seems experimental. Unless you were connected to a larger facility with specialized knowledge, harm could have ensued. I grew up in a rural areas. I didn't have experts in the field guiding my care. Fortunately, I have a mother who is a physician who recognized NF as a possibility but protected me from poking and prodding. She recognized that children vary in their development and let mine unfold. My mom believed in me.

Knowledge has expanded to the benefit of children growing up today. Their surveillance is levelheaded, guided by facts. We now know most cases of NF are mild and NF is common. Incidence is estimated to be 1:3,000 people worldwide (Maani, Westergard, Yang, Scaranelo, and Telesca, et al. 2019). There are many of us. "It is estimated that more than 100,000 Americans have NF, making it more common than cystic fibrosis, Duchenne muscular dystrophy, and Huntington's disease combined" (Suna 2016, 3).

Neurofibromatosis Type 1 is a result of a genetic change on chromosome 17 and specifically the NF1 gene. Normally, the NF1 gene directs production of the neurofibromin protein, explains the National Institute of Health (2020). "Neurofibromin acts as a tumor suppressor, which means that it keeps cells from growing and dividing too rapidly or in an uncontrolled way" (National Institute of Health, Genetic Home Reference 2020, 1–2). A genetic change on the NF1 gene allows tumors to grow unchecked along nerve pathways throughout the body.

Of all neurofibromatosis cases, 50 percent are a result of inheritance. The other 50 percent are spontaneous changes to the DNA "not resulting from anything that occurred in pregnancy" (Suna 2016, 7). Neurofibromatosis Type 1 has an autosomal dominant pattern of inheritance. This means that an affected parent has a 50 percent chance of passing it to offspring, explains the NIH (2020, 2). Gene expression (behavior) of neurofibromatosis varies between individuals (NIH) and even between individuals within the same family, adds the National Organization for Rare Disease (2017). Meaning NF impacts me differently than it impacts you.

Though "85–90 percent of people with NF1 will never develop a malignant tumor related to neurofibromatosis" (Suna 2016, 5), NF places individuals at a higher risk for other benign and malignant cancers (Maani et al. 2019). "The increased risk of breast cancer in NF1 has now been reported by numerous groups including a recent review of the literature" (Maani 2019).

Knowledge of breast cancer's association with NF was not widely disseminated at the time of my diagnosis. I didn't know my risk was increased, thinking I was at risk only for rarer cancers. A lot was out of my control; there was also much in my control. I couldn't alter my genes, but I could be proactive in my health. I could eat right, exercise, maintain mental health, and seek a balanced life.

Hopefully my chances would improve if I set myself up for good health. This is why, five days following my fortieth birthday, I got my tail in for a screening mammogram. My CAL, present at my armpit since birth, held new significance. It shouted, "Be diligent!" Its presence is a saving grace.

Screening

S creening saved my life! I honestly did not sense the cancer growing in me. Breast cancer doesn't just happen to other women, it happened to me. One in eight women will develop breast cancer in her lifetime (American Cancer Society 2019, 3). Breast cancer does not run in my family. Get in for your routine screening; no excuses! Breast health screenings for patients with neurofibromatosis (NF) starts early. Research tells us that women with NF are much more likely to develop breast cancer before age fifty (Maani 2019). Frontline health care providers need to recognize the genetic changes that carry higher cancer risk. Genetic counselors and geneticists are wonderful resources who have the most up-to-date screening recommendations. Utilize these professionals; they are partners in the health-care team.

Genomic medicine is rapidly changing the delivery of health care. Genetic testing tailors care to the individual. Detecting those at higher risk for cancers allow for appropriately timed and proactive screenings. At the same time, we cannot lose sight of the person who happens to be human.

Knowledge of one's genetics potentially impacts life course, outlook, and happiness. For example, Brad and I always wanted more than one child. After learning I have NF, serious soul-searching took place. We considered another pregnancy's impact on me and the impacts NF might have on another child. We decided to move forward. Norah was born, and I cannot imagine life without her. What I'm saying is that a genetic diagnosis must not assign a life sentence. You are valuable just the way you are. Environment and choices impact genes in yet to be determined ways. Don't let genetics scare you.

I received a call from my genetic counselor in regard to my genetic test. She says we knew the test would show NF, but it also shows another change, this one with the ATM gene, and unfortunately it is not the kind that will give you any money. The ATM change impacts gene repair and placed me at a higher risk for breast cancer. What are the chances! I have always been a quick healer and look younger than my age, so this was kind of funny. With all seriousness, knowledge of this ATM gene change allowed my cancer specialists to mindfully select treatment.

Section 2
The Race

Double D

I n the same blue recliner in which he was lulled as a baby, I rocked my eight-year-old son. I reminisced the feeding schedule, the late nights, the frequent awakenings. I reminisced his soft hair and sweet smell on my cheeks and lips. Blake was growing into an athletic boy whose limbs now spilled from my lap. We sat in the dark.

"Do you remember having your tonsils removed and why you needed them out?" I asked.

"Because I snored," he replied. His tonsils were causing sleep apnea.

"Yes, you didn't need them anymore and they were causing a problem."

As I made sense of the cancer diagnosis, I needed to make sense of it in a way my children could understand. This meant I was about to have a candid discussion about breasts with my son.

He leaned in with quiet interest.

"That is the same way it is with my breasts," I explained. "I'm having them removed because they're causing me trouble. There's something growing inside this one"—I pointed to my left breast—"and it shouldn't be there. It will make me sick. I'll look different after the surgery. I'll look like Norah. These breasts have served their purpose. They fed you and Norah. Now I don't need them."

It was a farewell to the breast moment.

Just as this was a farewell moment, it was also a lighthearted moment. I dreamed up the idea that I could somehow borrow fat from my husband for reconstruction. One morning, I stroked Brad's cheeks, pretending to be a vampire, requesting some fat.

"You can't do that!"

"Why not? It's just fat!"

If I was taking jowl fat, Brad required I also take it from "here and here and here."

"Buddy! I don't want to be a DD!"

Blake overheard me telling this story. As one who could not believe his ears, he requested my retelling. We laughed and laughed. The dreamy idea provided lightheartedness with each retelling, delighted I shared with him, a boy. *No, Blake, borrowing fat from Daddy is not possible.*

I'm Writing a Book!

"**I**'m writing a book," I tell my mother. "I have the material."
"Journaling is therapeutic," she replied.

I proclaimed it was not simply journaling. "I'm writing a book ... seriously!"

Grandpa would be proud.

Grandfather was also an author who wrote *Surgeon on Iwo: Up Front With The 27th Marines,* which was later republished by Presidio Press as *Combat Surgeon.* I may not kill with spoken words or convincing arguments, but give me a pen and watch out! I wrote myself into being a reader.

Before internet, email, and Facebook, kids had pen pals and exchanged letters. Frequent moves while growing up resulted in a string of pen pals. And when I was upset with my mother, she'd receive my letters too. I'd journal regularly, recording what was on my mind. Heartaches, joys, and trip details all went into my journal. The burdens of my heart were written within notebooks. Journaling helped me cope with my dad's death. I used writing as a way of expressing exactly how I felt. I even got some coupons out of the deal at nineteen years of age when I wrote the manufacturer of Honey Bunches of Oats. It seems so silly now. I wanted them to revert to former packaging. The new bold packaging didn't represent how I felt when I ate the cereal. But hey, maybe they wanted a slice of the kids' cereal market.

This is not intended to be a how-to book but a "me too" book. In the midst of so many things out of my control, my creative appetite expanded. I needed to create. I needed to reach outside myself. I needed to write my story to help others. Creating meant I was showing up, contributing, and moving forward. My approach is ingrained by the philosophy of occupational medicine where I worked for years. This philosophy of care lent well to me. Value is placed on doing what you can. It is not all or nothing. It does, however, demand that you do something.

Wellness

Wellness is not to be without illness or injury, but to thrive and function in spite of them. Health is not just physical. Rather, it is the interaction between body, mind, spirit, and the social, which produce wellness or lack thereof.

Exercise provides a three-for-one. It meets the need of body, mind, and spirit. In my twenties, I was intense about my exercise regimen. I beat myself up and got bent out of shape if I missed a day. In my thirties, an active lifestyle became a replacement. Exercise meant chasing after my children, walking a mile on my lunch break, and fitting in some squats before returning to patients. The dumbbells remained stashed and unused in the corner of my office.

Approaching forty, I asked myself whether simply squeezing activity into my day was really satisfying. Could I step it up? No longer could I rely on my physical accomplishments of my twenties as a competitive swimmer and fitness fanatic. It was easy to set rigidly strict workout standards as a college student with only myself to look after. As a mother, wife, and professional, regimented exercise has serious energy and scheduling restrictions.

"I figured it out!" I tell a friend, referring to the discovery of how to exercise in the midst of competing demands. She thinks I should be a Beachbody coach. My approach is too gentle, I tell her. If my body doesn't want to go fast, there is a reason.

I already wake up at an insanely early hour, so waking half an hour earlier is no loss. I walk on the treadmill for twenty minutes. Some mornings it is a fast pace and others it is slower. It all depends on how I'm feeling. I alternate each day between legs, arms, and core, aiming for one hundred repetitions. On leg days, I do squats, ten sets of ten. On the next leg day I do lunges. Arms and core days are also based on sets, totaling one hundred repetitions. I use light weights and work all major arm groups. In only two weeks, my sets and balance improved. I no longer stabilized on the wall.

Listening to TED Talks keeps me looking forward to the treadmill. When my mind gets going, so do my legs. The workout is completed in thirty to forty minutes, and my entire morning moves more smoothly. I'm on the ball! Breakfast, shower, coffee, backpacks, the kids are up, and we're out the door.

Exercise has a rightful place in the prevention and treatment of depression. I have experienced its positive benefits firsthand.

Mental health is my main motivation for exercising. I feared cancer might break my momentum or cause depression. I wanted to keep feeling my best. This is why I kept moving my body, even when it became painfully slow and short.

Norms 4

A cancer diagnosis breaks social norms and old patterns. Nothing will get in the way when life is on the line. Apprehension fades away; niceties fade away. There is no choice but to move forward. I was afraid. Yet inside me raged a fire, an animal on the prowl. I was not going to let them drop the ball—meaning laid back northern Minnesota. Things move along at a slower pace up here. Commitment and follow-through is just different than in a metropolitan area. *You will not dismiss me,* ran though my head. *You will not ignore me and think this is okay. I expect timely care; I expect follow-through.* My fight-or-flight was in fight mode; my life depended on it. Mark, my surgeon, was first to join my team. He set the tone and lowered my defenses.

I went alone but dressed in a special type of armor. I clothed myself in my friend Krista's purple scarf, the heart necklace given by my husband, and my new "let's conquer winter" parka. A mastectomy was inevitable. My mind was made up; I wanted

Mark to complete the surgery. I just asked that he save the birthmark under my left armpit.

"I'll do what I can but won't jeopardize the surgery," he replied.

I knew Mark professionally and selected him personally. His philosophy of care was more than I anticipated.

"I'm sorry you have to go through this," he began, grasping my hands and sitting close.

My shell cracked. Those tears were not of fear but of being overwhelmed by kindness. Things would be okay. I would receive the care and compassion I needed. As a health-care provider, I was not accustomed to being on the receiving end of caring and kindness.

Lastly, my surgeon emphasized, "If there is something you need, don't go around dropping hints. Be direct; ask for it."

At the conclusion of this well-guided visit, I needed a food hug. I went directly to the Wild Hare, my favorite bistro and coffeehouse in Bemidji, Minnesota, and ordered the usual. The way the Swiss cheese and caramelized onions meld together with the ham and warm oatmeal bread really does feels like a sandwich hug. Accompanying the perfect sandwich is the most delicious latte, served in a solid pottery mug, and topped with a crafted feather design.

Best Thing

I heard someone's story on the radio a long time ago. Half listening, I recall him saying cancer was the best thing that happened to him. *What an interesting idea*, I'd thought. But this was just an idea—until you experience it. Relationships repair and relationships grow, life is lived out-loud, without hesitation, boldly. Goals are renewed, priorities cemented. You get out of your head and realize there is nothing to lose. In the weeks following diagnosis, I never felt more alive. I was truly present, purposeful, and generous, and I cared less about people-pleasing. Cancer shook things up.

Before, I didn't have the guts to get a pixie cut. Now, I went for it. *If I don't like it, oh well. It will eventually fall out.*

"I have breast cancer," I bravely told my stylist, Anna. "Tomorrow I have my port placed."

Anna gave me the gift of a stylish cut, short on one side and long on the other. I wore this spunky cut for a month before it fell out at an alarming rate. The more my hair fell, the stronger my urge to pull at it. There had to be a point where it would stop falling. No! There was no stopping it. Krista was given the honor of shaving my head at the point of no return. This cements a friendship as no other. The adjectives beautiful, warrior, bad (in a good way), smart, and brave were used to describe this new bald look. These adjectives were empowering. I was more than a cancer diagnosis and was out to disprove the image of the sickly cancer patient. I did things a "sick cancer patient" isn't supposed to do. I planned for life.

Hyped up on adrenaline and willpower, I planned a trip. This would be waiting at the end of chemotherapy number six. I nested. The first thing was to straighten that annoying, crooked curtain nagging at me from a misplaced rod. I took hold of the ugly, stinky kids bathroom. It served as the main bathroom and one I was not comfortable having guests use. With the help of Pinterest, Home Depot, and Wayfair, I planned and executed my ideal bathroom. Before my hands began to shake, I painted walls. I convinced Brad that repurposing the linen armoire, sawing off its legs, and moving it into another room's closet was a good idea. My urging is very convincing. This was my cancer project.

I went on two weekend camping trips with Krista and our kids, strategically placed during the third week following chemotherapy.

"You're going tenting with the Katie who has cancer?" someone asked Krista.

"Yes. She's pretty amazing."

The Nurse

Learning the upcoming mastectomy would not require a hospital stay was one of the happiest days since diagnosis. As a nurse, I had it all planned out. I knew the risks of being hospitalized and of potential serious complications. I did not want to become another casualty, succumbing to a nosocomial (hospital acquired) infection. I knew the importance of hand hygiene and knew firsthand the complacency that sometime results from high-pressure, demanding, and overtaxing hospital work.

In my mind, I had it all worked out. I planned to take the bottle of Purell from my office into my hospital room, position it on my tray-top table, and motion over to anyone caught not "foaming in." Not a word, no accusations required; they would be personally sanitized. This extensive plan was not required. However, I still brought my sanitizer along to the surgery center. I probably looked strange, toting Purell around as a comfort item. At this point, I really didn't care. That Purell was what I needed.

To their credit, my nurses completely understood and gracefully humored me. Frankly, I did not care what the others thought. "Really?" was the snottiest response I encountered. What arrogance to assume I'm just another germophobic, anxious, over-reactive nurse. Little did she know of me and my tolerance for mud and the outdoors—not to speak of the rotting food kept in my bottom desk drawer. Carrying that Purell bottle kept me in charge of what little I could. Nosocomial infections kill! It is not just about wound infections, it's more about flu, pneumonia, strep, MRSA, and C-diff. The downward spiral of fighting one of these on top of cancer is the point.

"We found the cancer in the lymph nodes," Mark told me with compassion and calmness into my anesthesia-induced state of dulled awareness. I was being swept toward a longer road, one I knew was possible but not very likely. I returned home to the healing sanctuary I created in the far end of the house, surrounded by my favorite things and the encouraging reminders that I'm loved.

Lady Gaga demonstrates the ache and confusion that ensues when faced with what seems like an unsurmountable situation. I identified with her song "A Million Reasons." It was as if she knew how I felt. When the world comes crumbling down, giving you a million reasons to quit, you bow down and pray. Lord, be with me, show me the way. I have more than one reason to hang on. Please let me stay.

Treatment

7

This was all surreal. I thought cancer would amount to a little bump in the road. I would shake the dust off and keep moving forward. I felt healthy and strong. I wasn't sick, I just had cancer. To my dismay, six rounds of poisonous blasting aimed at fast-growing cells were required. Subjecting myself to poison to make myself well was counterintuitive. Here's the thing: I didn't feel sick, and forty is young.

Would people wonder what I did to bring this on? As a health nut, food was my medicine. My lifestyle was squeaky clean. Secretly though, I sometimes feel like Willy Wonka, the deprived dentist's child with an affinity for Mike and Ike and gummy bears. In all reality, candy did not bring cancer on. It is what it is.

I was told to pack for an all-day event, so I did. On chemotherapy day number one, some of the leisure items that filled three bags included books, a computer, phone, journal, coloring book, warm clothes, and a blanket. It appeared as if I was going on a trip, but to a destination unknown and one that couldn't be good. I waited in line with the other brave souls who were noticeably more seasoned; they did not have three bags and were not hysterical.

Brad planned to join me shortly after check-in. So there I was, standing alone with these three bags and seeing people I recognized from having worked in a department just down the hall. I felt out of place, on the other side, like it or not. I was standing with strangers who probably had a story similar to mine, maybe a story that would not end well. It was more than I could handle. Soon the dear women ahead of me noticed my grief and offered a comforting hug. We were in this together.

We're in This Together

Y ou'd think the oncology unit would be a sad, dismal
place. I'm here to tell you it's a very intentional place.
Everyone waiting in that lobby is on a mission. The process
is humanizing. I recognized how important relationships and
interactions are. I get attached. My treatment team at Joe Lueken
Cancer Center became my rock. Their attention to detail said,
"I've got you." With every treatment, I became less of me and
more of me. Routines, jobs, eyebrows, eyelashes, and status quo
slowly eroded away; the things that allude to a finished product
were stripped away. Without a choice, you are forced to move
forward just as you are.

Everyone Has Their Stuff

On my last day, chemotherapy number six, I arrived for the early appointment before the doors unlocked. By now, this was old hat and I traveled light.

A car drove up and parked by the door where I waited. A man got out and, with care, brought a wheelchair around for his wife. They appeared to have been married for quite some time and she didn't look well. My heart went out. Now I was the veteran. We are stripped down with this disease called cancer. It was my turn to offer human compassion just as the woman did for me on my first day.

This was her first round, and she was entering an unknown world. I don't remember our exact words or context, but we saw each other. Offering one's present self is sometimes all there is, and that can mean the most. What I do remember was seeing her uncomfortable arm and telling her how sorry I was.

She responded, "Everyone has their stuff, dear."

Stuff

I don't have to tell you that chemotherapy has side effects. Everyone is different. For me, it was three-week cycles of being hyper, rung out, and zoned out, followed by one week of feeling "normal." Repeat times six.

It's hyper like you've had too much caffeine, leaving you wishing for a reversal agent.

It's the type of diarrhea that has you running into a random Walmart bathroom, but it is closed for cleaning. You plead, "It's an emergency!" It's the intensified and overstimulated nerves, like frayed wire, that have you wanting to jump out of the car because you cannot stand the screeching little turkeys riding in back. Our family road trip theme song could easily be 2CELLOS' driving rendition of "Welcome to the Jungle."

Chemotherapy's impact runs deeper than physical implications. As each treatment option revealed itself, I faced strong-willed, internal resistance. Would the treatment outweigh its harms? What were the consequences of treatment? But really, what was the consequence of doing nothing? I reluctantly visited with Ethan, my radiation oncologist. Again, trust was built. He skillfully presented the facts of my cancer and the latest recommendations. Risks can be modified. Ultimately, the choice was mine.

I sat with six-year-old Norah, having a mother-daughter lunch at the Wild Hare. I had been laboring over the necessity of radiation following the chemotherapy.

Absorbing her innocence, cheer, and all her sweetness, I blurted, "Oh, Norah, there is nothing I wouldn't do for you."

Right there was my answer. I was not just living for myself; people counted on me. I couldn't risk being taken from my precious children and husband. I chose to act on the knowns rather than be stifled by fears and hypothetical complications. Knowledge is power and lessens fears.

What to do was made clear that day. However, sacrifice was really what was being asked. Sacrifice to outcomes unknown, sacrifice of my body, sacrifice of control. By that point I was feeling emotionally and physically naked. It's awful to say, but I felt like a boneless, skinless chicken straight out of a plastic wrapper. With everything stripped away and exposed, I imagined Jesus felt this way when he was crucified. God in human flesh understood the suffering of this world. He could understand mine.

Parenting

Without a doubt, this cancer journey has impacted the lives of my children. Though their lives moved along fairly normally, I hope it makes them better, more compassionate individuals. For starters, I hope they respect their bodies and the bodies of others. I hope they will treasure and respect relationships and have gratitude. I hope they saw their mother being brave and that taught them valuable lessons for meeting challenges in their own lives.

Because of chemo, I felt lacking as a parent, an inability to keep up. Mothers are like ringmasters and cattle herders. I couldn't muster this intensity. Blake and Norah are like rambunctious puppies. Saving my children from their next antic created intense anxiety. I felt guilty for wanting to be by myself, have quiet, listen to TED talks, and just read. I didn't want to be alone with them, these very active and noisy children. Their needs ran contrary to mine. Would I ever enjoy being alone with them again? Deceitful chemo brain! Cancer, you snake! Chemo brain left me questioning my abilities, forgetful, indecisive, and anxious. I took a break from writing during most of chemotherapy. My thoughts were random, disjointed, and far from eloquent.

Out of my necessity and theirs, Blake and Norah attended a summer program three days a week. The other days we spent with Brad or my friend Krista at the beach or at the movie theater. Mutually enjoyable activities were sought after. We watched a ridiculous number of box-office movies that summer. Time with Krista at the beach allowed me to let my guard down and enjoy my children. Krista and I sat as our children joyfully entertained each other. I'm eternally grateful for the faithful friend and husband who shared parenting with me.

Fargo

Fargo was a time for picking up the pieces, the beginning of a resurrection. I wasn't afraid of radiation as it couldn't be worse than chemotherapy. This was a time to reset, to start climbing out of the rubble. Terrified, I left my family for seven weeks. Grandma Bonnie beautifully filled the womanly void. I rested easy knowing she was there. Radiation was my job during the week. I went home on weekends. Terry was my angel, the one person I knew in Fargo. She opened her home and offered friendship.

I made my way through this phase, just as my friend Cathy knew I would. "Just think of all the people you'll reach," she said, endorsing her confidence in my ability to uniquely relate to those around me.

Fargo did not impress me at first. It was a barren, concrete maze of construction and retail, and I was a tiny, unknown speck wandering through this foreign place. By week two I was opened to the possibility that I could find my way around this city. Little by little I needed GPS less and less until this place became mine—there's my coffee shop, there's my mall, there's my gym, here's my route to treatment. These are places, but people made these places mine.

"Please pick up lefsa for the party," Terry asked. Lefsa is a Norwegian flatbread.

I set out to find this random place, with a side entrance, within a metal building, in the industrial part of town. There, I found Freddy's Lefsa and left with two packages because Brad and I like it too.

The next Thursday, I left with three packages and commented to the woman who served me that this is turning out to be a Thursday tradition. The following Thursday I entered the small, plain room attached to the kitchen. At the tiny counter was another women. Again, my lefsa order was served up in neat packages taken from a small cardboard box with that day's goods. *I missed her*, I noted. Leaving the building, I looked around. There she was! She was at the other end of the building getting out of her car.

"See you next week," she called.

"See you next week," I answered, waving out my car widow.

Humanity

As I waited for a radiation treatment, I noticed a women walk in. She was a former patient and was visiting her treatment team. She asked specifically for her "her girls" at the registration desk. Her companions were not there. Their chairs were vacated and now sat their replacements.

The woman's disappointment was palpable. Where did they go? Their names and whereabouts were unknown. To this patient, these care coordinators were more than names and more than the front-desk staff. To this patient, they meant the world. I imagined those coordinators smiling and greeting this women each morning, as mine did for me. They were probably her community, a constant in an otherwise unfamiliar and unpredictable environment.

Connections like this are what I miss about Fargo. I adore the women who administered the radiation that zapped any stray cancer cells. I call them my A-team. Monday through Friday, radiation was the highlight of my day. These women became friends, women I could cry on who welcomed my tears of worry and burden. They impacted my life by their presence. It is said that it is not what you say that people remember but how you make them feel. A-team saw me as more than a cancer patient.

We shared small nuances of life over these brief moments over thirty-three days. We shared our adventures in motherhood, discussed routines, places, and the changing of seasons. They found amusement in my routines following the day's treatment. I was on a vacation from my real life. "Swimming laps today" I'd tell them. Swimming is not recommend, Ethan would tell you. I didn't seek permission until one day I let it out, telling him I stopped swimming because it hurt to peel my tight one-piece Speedo swimsuit off my burnt chest. His eyes said it all: *I can't believe this woman.*

Scars

The saleswoman at my favorite women's store is a self-proclaimed expert at trickery, a skill acquired through decades of dressing to conceal her large chest prior to a breast reduction. She took it upon herself to help with my opposite issue.

"Accessorize, accessorize, accessorize," she says. Scarves, loose and busy tops, and jewelry distract the eye from the problem.

My blank canvas of a breastless chest jumped out as nakedness in the conservative tailored clothing I was accustomed to wearing. These clothes did not look right. However, the V-necks, long necklaces, and draping scarves suggested breasts. She tried to help me feel beautiful and womanly, to own a new look. I was happy to have new pieces of clothing. However, I did not leave the store feeling whole. I liked my sporty, sassy look and did not want to give that up. I was given a task to fool and hide what was missing. I did not want to reinvent myself or spend time pretending.

"Oh, wow! Look at those beautiful scars," the woman at the breast prosthesis store said. "The redness will fade nicely."

This was what I needed to hear, validation. Beauty comes in more than one form. She helped me pick out a comfortable size A and paid attention to detail. The breast prosthesis was right for me. Honoring myself, I did not want another extensive surgery to have breasts that I really didn't need. Did you know a back muscle can become a breast? Some women will go to this extent. Reconstruction is an individual choice. I choose to live flat. I prefer strength and a back over a breast. I happen to love my strong back and shoulders. I don't want to risk losing strength and ability for vanity's sake. I'd be heartbroken if I could not swim or paddle or portage or pack.

Advice

I'm hesitant to give advice because I'm sensitive to the uniqueness present in each individual's race. Here are the three most important points I offer you.

1. Find a coordinated treatment team you trust. They will form a cocoon around you.
2. Find projects that enhance and entertain your body, mind, and spirit. Keep moving forward.
3. Don't shut yourself off from others. Don't pretend. You are giving a gift by showing up just as you are.

Why do we pretend so? Pretending means we go through this world not knowing what struggle looks like or what to do about it. We have no example. Consequently, we convince ourselves we are an anomaly and alone when we struggle.

I looked for Paula. A few years earlier I noticed her, working at her bagel store. She wore a head scarf, greeting customers and tending her store. I thought, *What an amazing woman. She must have cancer, and look at all she's doing!* With my diagnosis, I thought of Paula. She was the only one I'd seen living in the midst of a diagnosis similar to mine. *Where was she?* I frequented Big Apple Bagels, hoping that one day our paths would cross. And eventually they did! Following her example, I wore my favorite purple sports cap. No hiding behind a wig.

Helping

My friend Aiden approached me and explained that a friend of hers has cancer. She didn't know what to do. "Should I bring it up?" she asked. "I don't want to offend her."

I suggested she bring it up. She is on a survival mission. Cancer is forefront in her mind. It is all very real. Acknowledge the associated struggle. She'll likely welcome your concern. Say things like, "I can imagine (fill in the blank) is difficult. How are you doing with that?"

"I can't imagine" is a pet peeve of mine. It really means "I'm afraid to imagine." It's isolating. Try to imagine. Be present in those struggles. A "me too" goes a long way.

It doesn't have to be huge. See a need, fill it! Little things go a long way and will stick with a cancer survivor forever.

"Can I meet you at the surgery center and pray with you before surgery?" my friend Gay asked. She showed up even before the sun rose. "It's Easter. Do you mind if I pick out treats for Blake and Norah?"

Oh, Gay! You don't know what this meant. Your caring for my children was caring for me. My mother's heart could not do it all.

Be intentional and consistent. Krista made me a new soup each week of my cancer treatment. This brought so much love and support. It said, "I've got your back and I'm on this journey with you. I'm not afraid to be present and I will love you regardless."

Cathy consistently sent notes of encouragement, reminders of God's love, care packages, and an abundant source of coffee money. She is the friend who is up for the challenge even when it is completely out of her realm. She is the friend, without children, who I asked to make an emergency Target run for nursing bras after Blake was born, when my breasts were bursting at the seams. He was my first child, and I was not prepared. Cathy nailed it.

This time, when Cathy asked what I needed, my requests were a silk pillow case and head scarves. She didn't bat an eye. Again, she nailed it. As a friend, this said, "I'm not afraid to enter this struggle with you."

Aiden, who asked the framing question, took my suggestions to heart. Every week she wrote her high school friend whom she'd not seen in years. When Aiden showed up for her friend's surprise fortieth birthday party, it was clear how much those letters meant. Aiden sent me a picture of this friend and her, clearly bonded. I'm so proud of these women, the one who ran the race and the faithful fan.

The Finish Line

What do we make of the times when prayers, hope, encouragement, and reasons for living are not enough? Death happens anyhow and it seems so unfair. Sarah's journey started when I was in the middle of my race. I was about to have my fourth infusion when she was diagnosed with ovarian cancer. Sarah and I ran track together in high school. Now, as adults, mothers, and wives we ran the cancer race. Our children are the same ages and full of abundant energy and spirit. I did not want her to feel alone. At the same time, I too was afraid of saying the wrong things. Most of all I wanted Sarah to feel validated.

As I began the recovery phase of this endurance event, it became clear that Sarah was not doing well and our paths were diverging. I was rebuilding life, going back to work, and getting my first haircut as she faded physically. Oh how I wished Sarah could be by my side! Sarah accepted her demise as hard it was to imagine a world for Mike and their boys without her in it. She loved her family and her work. She lived her faith clearly. Her life, acceptance of death, and confidence in the resurrection are a testimony to the power of Christ in her life.

Mike reminds us that while we live in this world, brokenness, sadness, and death happen to all without discrimination. It is the universal condition of living in this world. God understands, he grieves, and he sent help. Jesus conquered the grave, and because of that we have hope. Eternity starts now.

Sarah crossed the ultimate finish line into the mystery that lies ahead. She ran an exceptional race. "Well done, my good and faithful servant" (Matthew 25:23 New Living Translation).

I wept over Sarah's death. It could easily have been me. Speaking to her spirit, I promised to finish this book. I would press on.

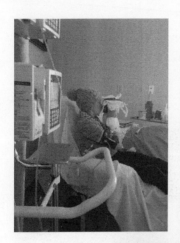

Section 3

Recovery

Rubble

1

The finish line approached with every cancer-zapping treatment. Radiation was the last leg of the race. Recovery was just around the bend. And then, boom! Round thirty-three was completed. Chapter closed. Climbing out of the rubble.

The race left me a wet noodle, a mess of physical, mental, and emotional exhaustion. Climbing out of the rubble meant ordering my life again. Sara Groves' song "Less like Scars" speaks to this. Her song feels meant for me. Cancer made for a very hard year; it rearranged everything. Then, with healing practically unnoticeable, hope rose. I listened to this song over and over on my daily commute through thirty-three insanity-provoking stoplights from West Fargo to Roger Maris Cancer Center in downtown Fargo. It uplifted me. Could life look better than this?

Recovery

Healing is subtle. Recovery is one step in front of the other. Recovery is honing patience with one's self. Recovery is taking pleasure in small strides forward. Recovery is finding courage.

Brené Brown, research professor at University of Houston, brilliantly articulates her findings in her TED talks. In her talk "Listening to Shame," she states, "Vulnerability is our most accurate measurement of courage" (March 2012, 4:31). She adds, "Vulnerability is not weakness. … Vulnerability is the birthplace of innovation, creativity, and change" (5:45).

To let ourselves be seen starts with believing, "I am enough" (June 2010, 19:39). Brené's findings greatly influenced my recovery. She encouraged me to show up just as I was, reenter "into the arena" before I was "bulletproof." Joy grew as I showed up. As strength and endurance in all areas of life increased, my gratitude overflowed.

I'm grateful for the experiences that trained me for the race, friendships, and outpouring of love that sustained me, and gratitude that I survived. First and foremost, I was grateful for the resilience and gratitude emanating from me. When my survival was unknown, I'm grateful I could say, "No matter what happens, I've lived a good life." This outpouring feels supernatural, leaving me convinced God's spirit is working through me. God's presence weaving through my entire life has never been so clear.

Cancer departments hold a bell-ringing tradition. When a patient finishes treatment, he or she rings a large brass bell for all to hear. It's a big deal. For the ringer, it's a sigh of relief; for the hearer, it signals hope. As the hearer, I was reminded that this too shall pass and that someday I could be ringing the bell.

As the bell ringer, hope became reality. On October 4, 2018, I rang the bell, signaling the completion of radiation. On March 19, 2019, my treatments were complete and I rang the cancer bell for the final time at Joe Lueken Cancer Center. One year of treatment was complete; I fulfilled the process laid out by my health-care providers. Ringing the bell felt like graduation. Remember, however, graduation doesn't close a book; it indicates the next chapter may begin. The next steps were up to me.

One Word

With each new year, my friend Cathy and I each pick one word to represent a theme and focus. Our selected words are not New Year's resolutions. Feelings of failure ensue when resolutions and willpower fade. Choosing a theme releases that guilt and shame. Jon Gordon, Dan Britton, and Jimmy Page wrote about this theme-based approach in *One Word That Will Change Your Life* (2012), the book that gave Cathy and me our inspiration.

The authors' aim is to demonstrate that weaving a chosen word or theme into life brings meaningful changes. One year I chose the word *simple* and branched out its meaning. I delved in immediately, simplifying my physical surroundings and purging items that were no longer useful. These items often took up space and attention. In regard to my wardrobe, for example, it meant maintaining a classy, sporty look. In my profession, it meant streamlining tasks and documentation.

My work desk became uncluttered and functional. "Simple" reduced the distractions in my life.

Fresh was 2018's word. Fresh was alive and well. By February, I had plans for a new job with fresh opportunities, fresh setting, fresh learning, and fresh people. It would be an escape from what had become a soul-sucking job.

All seemed to crash downward with the cancer diagnosis. "Fresh" was ripped away and replaced with *survive*. Plans changed. Looking back, "fresh" still wove its way throughout that cancer year. To fully embrace "fresh," every common, ordinary, and guaranteed aspect of life must first be stripped away. Cancer did that. It slowly stripped away old ways of being.

Live would be my word for 2019. Again, in retrospect, you cannot go from broken to living by simply posting a new calendar. It too is a slow process. I reluctantly use the word "broken," but it most accurately describes cancer's impact. Broken is not shattered beyond repair. No! Broken is mendable.

I've learned that living and mending take courage, and 2019 was a courageous year.

Live

My application of 2019's word "live" started with several questions. How do I speak to myself and others? How do I build a stronger body? What things will I let enter my life? What has this all meant? How will it impact my life? Being broken down means I can build back stronger; that was what I aimed to do.

To signal this move forward, I made a box. Inside and out, I plastered my cancer artifacts and placed letters of encouragement inside. I was ready for the hard work ahead. Cancer treatment does not just dump you at the end of the road with a "go live happily ever after." Recovery takes work; little recognition is given to its lengthy process. Recovery is solitary work, emotional, physical, and spiritual work.

Recovery is ultimately an intimate walk with God. Exercise and music are my tools. Exercise is cathartic. It helped me purge complex feelings; gratitude, fear, and hope were expressed on the treadmill and walks down country roads with hot, dirt-mixed tears streaming down my face. In these places, my thoughts and feelings had glimmering clarity. The book you are reading now came together partly as the result of "Siri, take note," spoken into my iPhone 7. Siri took notes while I moved on ski trails, dirt roads, and the treadmill. I'm brought to a higher level of awareness and communion with God through exercise. Exercise brings what is inside out. Don't be afraid of your feelings; let yourself feel whatever you feel. I learned this tool long ago with my dad; let the tears stream down as cleansing prayers to God.

I built a "power" playlist on iTunes and committed to an early morning routine of working out six days a week. Yes, it became an intentional, regimented exercise routine with an even mix of strength training and cardio. I was tired of feeling physically weak. I pushed myself to get physically strong and am now benching more than ever before. Exercise is also a practice in mindfulness as one focuses on the current set and each individual repetition. This is how exercise can be fun. You just have to tune out the unending to-do list and worries running on repeat through your head. Strong arms, chest, shoulders, and back are rewards. Strong mind and emotions are my prize.

My playlist keeps me motivated and encouraged. It includes Lauren Daigle's "You Say"; "Fight Song" by Rachel Platten; "Brave" by Sara Bareilles; "Scars to Your Beautiful" by Alessia Cara; and "Try Everything" by Shakira. These songs help defeat negative self-talk and doubts. They remind me of the Creator, who uplifts and claims me.

I'm not defined by my struggles. My life counts and I can do great things. I will take back my life. Rachel Platten describes the strength of the human spirit as a fire burning deep within. The human spirit is resilient. Bareilles tells me to live out loud; the world wants to see my courage. Lauren Daigle tells me I'm stronger than my own assessments.

Alessia Cara shows me pretending is futile. Life scars are what makes us beautiful. The world needs us to be real. Scars are beautiful both literally and figuratively.

Bridge

This is my metaphor for transition: Imagine crossing a bridge. This shows the movement away from a season of need. When my dad died, I walked around in a state of grief and self-absorption until one day, I felt God whispering, "It's time to look outside yourself."

It's the same way now. I've worked in a new department for more than a year now. Feeling like a novice was uncomfortable. At the same time, it offered positive challenges to perfect my processes, learn, and better my craft. It stimulated my brain and slowly stripped away the cobwebs and chemo fog. My craft is healing and guiding. Recovery is building back this part of me.

People wonder if life is different after beating cancer. They assume I have new prospective, priorities, or sage wisdom. Was there a lesson I needed learning? For a year, I was fixated on this, looking for that magical transformation. The stubborn part of me wanted to believe that cancer didn't have to teach me a thing. In reality, I now have greater depth to my prospectives. Life is not peaches and cream, life has returned to, well, usual. It is swept back up into the typical.

You'd think I'd be more excited and immune to negativity and frustration. I wanted life, with all its frustrations, so badly when it was potentially being stripped from me. This is all I really wanted: to referee the roughhousing between Blake and Norah, homework fights, parent-teacher conferences, carting the kids to activities, putting healthy meals together, and coordinating professional responsibilities with home responsibilities, laundry and dishes. Life still holds the usual worries, including making sure our kids grow up to be kind and capable adult humans. The practicalities include making enough money to meet our needs and some desires.

Somewhere well into 2019, I recognized that my goal of whole-person recovery was a reality. I believe enduring these events resulted in a better version of myself. I still wrestle with the universal human conditions requiring love and belonging. I'm not impervious to other's opinions, nor can I do life on my own. Cancer was not supposed to fix me or make for a blissful, happily-ever-after life. It has, however, facilitated a love that allows me to live more fully. My story continues.

As I seek wholehearted living, I offer these principles gleaned from my endurance event.

1. Live authentically.
2. Live generously.
3. Try new things.

4. Look up.
5. Relationships matter; love lasts.

"We can rejoice, too, when we run into problems and trials, for we know that they help us develop endurance. And endurance develops strength of character, and character strengthens our confident hope of salvation. And this hope will not lead to disappointment. For we know how dearly God loves us, because he has given us the Holy Spirit to fill our hearts with his love" (Romans 5:3–5 New Living Translation).

Final Thoughts

Remember Officer Judy Hopps, the main character in the movie *Zootopia*? This spunky character did not take no for an answer. She mustered willpower and courage, and when challenged, kept going. I felt like Officer Hopps, "hopping" my way through this cancer journey. Shakira sang the cover song, "Try Everything." This song inspires me and continues to do so. "Try Everything" means to me trying before having it all figured out beforehand.

I don't know what try everything means for you. You may have tried everything to win this cancer fight. I'm well aware that surrendering to death is a poignant reality for many of my sisters. I'm sorry for the grief this causes when it ends this way for you or someone you love. Please know that whatever you go through, nothing can separate us from the love of God (Romans 3:38–39 New Living Translation).

Writing this book helped me process and move forward. It was written in real time with the hope it would someday be of help and encouragement to others. Although our journeys don't look the same or end in the same ways, I hope parts resonate with you. Speaking truthfully about my life, though uncomfortable, is my gift to you. May you not feel alone.

As I edit and revise, we are in the midst of the COVID-19 pandemic. 2020 has involved uprise and general unrest. Our entire world aches. Individuals ache personally from uncertainty and confusion. When will this all end and what will life look like after?

I see parallels between my cancer journey and what is happening now. Just like cancer, there is fear at first. Then comes the pain of treatment. We are asked to do life in ways like never before. People are pulling together and thinking outside the box. We are learning new ways of schooling our children, working, serving each other, and worshiping. We evaluate the busy schedules we once had. Sometimes we long for them. When our world starts recovering, I hope it becomes a better one.

Bibliography

Breast Cancer Facts and Figures 2019–20. Last accessed April 4, 2020. (Atlanta: American Cancer Society 2019.) https://www. cancer.org/content/dam/cancer-org/research/cancer-facts-and-statistics/breast-cancer-facts-and-figures/breast-cancer-facts-and-figures-2019-2020.pdf.

Brown, Brené. (March 2012). "Listening to Shame" (video file). https://www.ted.com/talks/brene_brown_listening_to_shame. html%20or/discussion.

_____. (June 2010). "Power of Vulnerability" (video file). Retrieved from https://www.ted.com/talks/brene_brown_the_power_of_vulnerability?language=en

Caracciolo, Alessia, Felder, W., Tillman, C., Wansel, A., and Franks, J. "Scars to Your Beautiful" from *Know-it-All*. Def Jam Records, produced by Pop & Oak; Sebastian Kole; and DJ Frank E., 2015.

Children's Tumor Foundation Guide. Newly Diagnosed with NF1: A Guide to the Basics. Last accessed April 4, 2020. https://issuu. com/childrenstumor/docs/newlydiagnosedwithnf1guide-final.

Duckworth, Angela Lee. "Grit: The Power of Passion and Perseverance," TED Talk, April 2013. https://www.ted.com/ talks/angela_lee_duckworth_grit_the_power_of_passion_ and_perseverance/up-next?language=en

Dweck, Carol, October 2014. "Developing a Growth Mind-set." https://www.youtube.com/watch?v=hiiEeMN7vbQ.

Gaga, Lady, Ronson, M., and Lindsey, H. "Million Reasons," *Joanne*. Interscope Records, 2016.

Gordon, Jon, Britton, D., and Page, J. *One Word That Will Change Your Life* (Hoboken, New Jersey: Wiley 2013).

Groves, Sarah. "Less like Scars," *All Right Here* (Franklin, TN: Sponge Records 2002).

Lisney, Cameron. (September 2014). "Growth Mind-set." https:// www.youtube.com/watch?v=-_oqghnxBmY.

Maani, N., Westergard, S., Yang, J., Scaranelo, AM, Telesca, S., and Thain, E. (2019). "NF1 Patients Receiving Breast Cancer Screening: Insights from the Ontario High Risk Breast Screening Program." _Cancers_ May 2019; 11(5): 707. doi: 10.3390/ cancers11050707. Last accessed April 4, 2020. https://www.ncbi. nlm.nih.gov/pmc/articles/PMC6562659/.

National Institute of Health; Genetic Home Reference. Neurofibromatosis Type 1. Last accessed April 4, 2020. https:// ghr.nlm.nih.gov/condition/neurofibromatosis-type-1#genes.

National Organization for Rare Disease. Neurofibromatosis Type 1. Last accessed April 4, 2020. https://rarediseases.org/ rare-diseases/neurofibromatosis-type-1-nf1/.

Platten, Rachel. "Fight Song," *Fight song*. Columbia Records, 2015.

About the Author

Katherine Friese is a nurse practitioner and also a cancer survivor. From this unique position, she candidly speaks about her life before cancer, her cancer fight, and cancer's impact. Through struggle she's found that endurance, character, and hope grow. Her storytelling and no-nonsense writing style invites inquiry and thoughtfulness. You will be uplifted and encouraged by her wholehearted story.